Beautiful America's

UTAH

Beautiful America's
UTAH

Photography by David C. Schultz

Text by Sena T. Flanders

Beautiful America Publishing Company
™

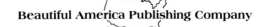

Front cover: Spring in Albion Basin, Wasatch Mountains

Opposite title page: Winter at the Sundial, Twin Peaks Wilderness Area

Published by
Beautiful America Publishing Company
P.O. Box 244
Woodburn, OR 97071

Library of Congress Catalog Number 00-034241

ISBN 0-89802-723-3
ISBN 0-89802-722-5 (paperback)

Printed in Korea

Contents

Mount Timpanogos and glacier in spring

Desert wildflower, White Canyon

Beautiful Deer Creek Lake

Introduction

A person must take a long pause before beginning to describe the state of Utah. Many thoughts jump to mind, and a few words in summation emerge — colors, variety, homogeny, growth, hot, cold, public, recreation, technology, heritage.

Utah, the square state with its northeast corner cut out, is a state whose environments and terrain show the full spectrum of the color wheel. In terms of the palette, the landscape represents cool shades in the north, where two major mountain chains intersect and hug the Great Salt Lake. An aerial view of the center of the state would show hues of beige, brown, pink and green as mountains give way to desert. Then in the south, as at the bottom of a fire, rough and deep canyons glow with shades of red and black with veins of blue, as waterways flow through the state to the Gulf of Mexico.

The variety of the state is best seen in its landscapes and its temperatures. It has mountain peaks that tower to 13,000 feet and play host to arctic temperatures. The briny wonder called the Great Salt Lake is a concentration of salinity so dense that it can be seen in infrared photographs from outer space. Valley floors that are irrigated blossom with greens in the summer. But they are surrounded by high desert climes that receive less than 10 inches of water per year and support little to no vegetation except that which comes forth immediately following spring showers. In contrast to the mountains, the arid valleys simmer to temperatures well over 100 degrees in the summer.

While the topography boasts variety, there is homogeny in the populace, mainly due to its heritage. The state is largely comprised of a caucasian population whose roots extend to the mid-1840s when the first wave of Mormon immigrants fled the eastern states to establish their idea of Zion.

That founding group of Latter-day Saint pioneers in 1847 was comprised of 143 men, three women and two children. News that they had found "the right place," as described by their leader Brigham Young when he first saw the Salt Lake Valley, spread east from where their tracks had come. Other bands of pioneers followed, and as nature had its way, as instructed by church leaders, the number of Mormons multiplied. As the valley was settled, its early inhabitants began to colonize outreaches of the area. This mass migration of 100,000 church members helped found 200 cities in the state.

Soon, the white man outnumbered the Native American who, up until the middle 19th century, had enjoyed what is now known as the intermountain United States. Those Native Americans prior to the mid-1840s had been able to savor the intermountain area as their own, except for a few Spanish explorers and brave mountain men.

Mountain men came in search of beaver pelts to help satisfy consumer demand in America and Europe. In the early 1820s, pelts brought $10 and more in the St. Louis market and other cities. To find the beaver, which were being depleted in the tributaries of the Columbia and Missouri rivers, mountain men had to push west. Their initial title for what is now Utah was the "land of the Yutas."

But the area's first known residents were the Anasazi, which means "ancient ones." These Pueblo people were here from about 1 A.D. to 1300. The Ute Tribe (hence the title Utah) inhabited the central and northern reaches of what would later become the state, while the Navajo Indians roamed the southern areas. The first significant non-Mormon residents of the territory were U.S. troops sent to Utah in 1858 and 1862. During the 1860s, however, non-Mormons, also known as "Gentiles" came in increasing numbers to engage in mining, business, religious and educational work.

As the second half of the 19th century rolled by, other ethnic groups moved into the state, comprising approximately 10 percent of the otherwise Mormon populace. The construction of a transcontinental railroad brought a mix of backgrounds, and so did the lure of mining. For example, in Park City, now an international ski destination, places such as the China Bridge Stairs and Swede Alley are still in use. The central Utah community of Price and Utah's capital city, Salt Lake, commemorate their heritage in Greek festivals each summer.

What transpired in Utah after pioneers arrived was in keeping with Mormon teachings: to multiply, and to make the desert blossom like a rose. Modern natives have been successful in fulfilling those directives. And they grapple with the consequences. Highways are choked with traffic due to the rapidly growing population. This surge of people was and is fueled by a Mormon penchant to have large families. Utah's growth outpaces the national average. More than 65 percent of the state's growth is attributed to natural increase from within its borders. The same percentage is expected to continue into the next couple of decades. Utah has the distinction of being ranked first in the nation for the largest household size, with three-plus people per home.

From a newcomer's perspective, Utah has become a very desirable place to live. People from crowded eastern states and California have been pulling up their stakes to move here. The state's assets are a draw: clean cities, industrial and commercial growth, a strong work ethic among employees, reasonable wage scales, comfortable climates, and seemingly endless recreational opportunities.

People in Utah take pride in their state, as if it were a public commodity that all support. And it is no

Winter at Devil's Castle, Little Cottonwood Canyon

Opposite: Mount Timpanogos from Timpanogos Basin

wonder ... Utah is one of only a few states in the nation that is largely "owned" by the public, and not just the public that lives in Utah, but the nation as a whole.

Various types of federal lands account for 72.6 percent, or 1,569,000 acres of Utah. Lands owned by the state itself account for 13.2 percent, or 300,600 acres. Since such a large percentage of the state is managed by federal agencies, the U.S. government is one of the largest employers in Utah. Agencies include the Bureau of Land Management, which oversees more than 22 million acres, the USDA Forest Service manages 9 million acres, and the National Park Service oversees almost 3 million acres.

The fact that so much of Utah is made available as parks and recreation areas for residents and visitors has led to a strong tourist economy that is admired worldwide. Tourism has eclipsed other economies that initially drew people, such as mining.

Utah was a stopping place in the gold rush of the 1840s. On their way west, many prospectors stayed and made their fortunes in gold and silver. Mansions and tall office buildings in downtown Salt Lake City bear testament to those who were most fortunate in their mining ventures.

The 1900s saw the extraction of huge quantities of copper from the Kennecott mine on the west side of the Salt Lake Valley, in the foothills of the Oquirrh Mountains. The enormous open-pit mine can be viewed by hundreds of air travelers each day who fly in and out of Salt Lake City International Airport. Kennecott continues to be one of the nation's most productive copper mines.

Coal mining is and has been a pillar of the economy in central Utah, particularly in the counties of Emery and Carbon whose heritage is tied to the black rock. Uranium mining, which fueled commerce in the dusty towns of southeastern Utah in the 1950s, '60s and '70s, has largely gone the way of gold and silver excavation—it is all but non-existent. Many made their livelihood on these precious natural resources. Many sustained their families. A few made fortunes.

Today, the livelihoods that provide the economic foundation for the state have moved away from the extractive industries. That foundation is now built on the service industry, government jobs, tourism, and high-tech business involving bio-medicine and computer software. While the nation as a whole faired well in creating jobs as it neared the millennium, Utah outpaced the national average. The state remains near the top in the nation for starting and growing a business, particularly the Salt Lake City/Provo area. And the poverty level in Utah ranks second to last among the states.

Employers find the state a successful business base in part due to their operating costs. For example, Utah ranks third lowest in the nation with respect to workers compensation costs. It has the lowest rate in the western United States.

Though meager populations first took up residence in the area that later became known as Utah, the number of people has rapidly multiplied. By the mid-1990s, the population had reached the 2 million mark. Head counters expect it to hit 3 million by about 2016. Still, in comparison with the rest of the country, Utah ranks about 35th in population.

People in Utah generally are younger and live longer than the nation as a whole. It has the youngest median age in the United States, and it ranks last out of 50 states in the percent of its population over 64 years old. The people of Utah may indeed live longer lives than those in other states, but percentage wise, this group of senior citizens is small.

Religiously, the state is still dominated by members of the Church of Jesus Christ of Latter-day Saints (LDS), also commonly referred to by themselves and by non-church members as the Mormons. About 65 percent of the people are members of the LDS Church statewide. Other religious groups, in order of size, are Methodist, Roman Catholic, Lutheran, Episcopalian, Presbyterian, Disciples of Christ, Baptist and Congregationalist.

Utahns have an appreciation for the fine arts. Performing organizations include Ballet West, the Mormon Tabernacle Choir, Pioneer Theater Company, Repertory Dance Theater, Ririe-Woodbury Dance Company, Utah Opera and the Utah Symphony. The southern Utah town of Cedar City each summer hosts what is recognized as one of the finest Shakespearean Festivals in the country.

In addition, there are many professional and amateur theater organizations, choruses and arts-oriented groups in the smaller communities across the state. During the Christmas season, one may either participate in or listen to a locally-produced rendition of Handel's "The Messiah" in most any corner of the state. The Utah Arts Council represents more than 400 organizations for performing, visual and literary arts.

While the state's fine arts are certainly an asset to its residents, what draws visitors are largely the outdoor recreation and scenic attributes.

Utah has 14 downhill ski resorts that in the winter time receive an average of 500 inches of snow. The state's white stuff has earned the moniker "Greatest Snow on Earth" due to its light consistency. The powder is the result of storm clouds passing over the Great Salt Lake on their way to the high peaks of the Wasatch and Uinta mountain ranges.

Utah has five national parks, seven national forests, six national monuments, two national recreation sites, and 48 state parks. It is home to the Utah Jazz, a National Basketball Association team, which were Western Conference champions in 1998 and 1997. The women's pro basketball team, the Utah Starzz, also

Sunset in the Wasatch Mountains near Alta

Wildflowers of the Timpanogos Wilderness Area

The Sundial, Lake Blanche area, Wasatch Mountains

15

calls the state home, along with the Salt Lake Buzz Triple-A baseball team and the Utah Grizzlies, an International Hockey League team.

Utah will also have 17 days of glory during February 8-24, 2002 when the state hosts the 2002 Winter Olympic Games. The Olympic Flag arrived in Salt Lake on February 24, 1998, officially proclaiming it an Olympic city. Although Salt Lake was given the Olympic title, very few of the Olympic venues are actually in the city. Also playing host are the Winter Sports Park near Park City, Park City Mountain Resort, Deer Valley, Soldier Hollow and Snow Basin Ski Area. Salt Lake is the largest city ever to host the winter games. Many of the venues are open for the public to enjoy.

Mount Timpanogos Cascade Cirque near Sundance

Salt Lake & The Wasatch Front

S alt Lake City serves as a great gateway to Utah. Though travelers come from its neighboring states—Wyoming, Nevada, Idaho, Colorado and Arizona—the capital city and the commerce associated with it are the biggest draw. Salt Lake International Airport and two major interstates are huge conduits for travel in the Salt Lake Valley.

The city is often called the "Crossroads of the West" due to its easy access by highway, rail and air. Interstates 15 and 80 and U.S. Highway 89 cut through the valley. Amtrak routes serve east and west by rail. By air, half of the U.S. population is within 2.5 hours. Salt Lake International Airport is a depot to nearly a dozen major carriers, and it is closer to the heart of the city than nearly any other airport in the country.

Salt Lake City sits at an elevation of 4,000 feet. It is uniquely situated to allow for a broad range of recreational opportunities. For example, on many spring days outdoor enthusiasts may choose between golf or skiing, or do both on the same day. In the summer temperatures hover in the 90-degree range, allowing for bountiful growing seasons for flowers and vegetables. Winters often coat the valley floor with snow, but the white stuff lasts only weeks there, as opposed to several months in the mountain ranges that tower nearby.

Visitors and residents alike will find the greatest concentration of cultural, recreational, educational and commercial opportunities in the Salt Lake Valley. However, the counties that stretch north and south from the capital city are growing at a rapid rate, as are the urban amenities that only a few decades ago could be found primarily in Salt Lake.

Salt Lake City's biggest claim to fame is perhaps its namesake. The large body of brine that lies west of the city is one of the earth's anomalies. Mountain men in the mid-1800s who trapped fur in the area first thought the inland sea was an arm of the Pacific Ocean. The extremely high concentrations of salt in the water are useful in commercial salt production and for brine shrimp harvesting, although that industry is scaling back due to concerns about the declining populations of the tiny shrimp.

The Great Salt Lake in the first half of the 1900s was home to a great ballroom-dancing castle known as Saltair. A roller coaster and arcade drew crowds that played on the shores and enjoyed swimming in the buoyant salt water. Now, Raging Waters is a popular water theme park, as well as Lagoon, just north of Salt Lake in Kaysville. Originally named for its location near a lagoon of the Great Salt Lake, the park features swimming pools, water slides, a pioneer village and oodles of thrilling rides for young and old alike. Lagoon is the largest amusement park between Kansas City and the west coast.

There are two major islands in the lake—Antelope and Stansbury. Both offer outdoor recreation opportunities in a remote setting, although the islands are very close to the densely populated Wasatch Front. Antelope Island is more than 28,000 acres in size. The park receives more than 250,000 visitors each year, and was once considered as a national park. Its diverse topography has been likened to both the Highlands of Scotland and the tundra of Alaska. Wildlife there includes bison, antelope, deer, bighorn sheep and countless migratory birds that depend on the lake for their survival. Recreationists enjoy mountain-biking, hiking and horseback riding. An annual buffalo round-up is held here in late October.

To access the island, visitors pay a fee to cross a causeway that connects the island with the mainland. When record amounts of precipitation fell in Utah in the mid-1980s, flooding caused the lake to rise to such a degree that the causeway was submerged.

Stansbury Island is also open to hiking and biking. Outdoor enthusiasts particularly enjoy it in the spring and fall when temperatures are moderate and the ground is snow-free. The island is accessible by automobile, and while it is called an island, there are mud flats and evaporative ponds on its south side that stretch across to the valley.

The Great Salt Lake in prehistoric times was much larger. What historians call Lake Bonneville actually covered all the valleys of the Wasatch Front, and the shoreline is still visible along the foothills of the valley. Walkers now enjoy footpaths along what is called the Bonneville Shoreline Trail.

Other more prominent features that beckon visitors to Salt Lake City are those related to the Mormon Church. Historic Temple Square lies in the heart of the city, and draws more visitors annually than any other tourist destination in the state. There is a full schedule of guided tours daily at Temple Square. Millions of colored lights in the trees transform the square into a Christmas wonderland each holiday season. Across the street is the LDS Family History Library. The library is available to the public for researching family lines.The library contains one of the largest repositories of genealogical records in the world and is free to the public.

As planned by early Mormon Church leader Brigham Young, Temple Square comprised the very center of the city from which roads extended outward. City blocks are arranged on a grid pattern in 10-acre squares, separated by streets 132 feet wide. This width was determined by Young as being "wide enough for a team of four oxen and a covered wagon to turn around."

Evening falls over sprawling Salt Lake City and the State Capitol building

The magnificent Mormon Temple in Salt Lake City

In 1999, the Salt Lake City Council sold one block of Main Street between Temple Square and the Joseph Smith Memorial Building to the LDS Church. Construction is underway on an underground parking garage, and landscaping including a large reflecting pool, to connect Temple Square with the block containing the church office buildings. One block north of Temple Square, the recently completed Assembly Hall building is used to supplement the old Tabernacle building, which pre-dates the Salt Lake Temple. The new Assembly Hall seats 21,000 people. It may well be the largest auditorium/theater in the world, covering almost all of a complete Salt Lake City block.

The Salt Lake Convention & Visitors Bureau explains that Salt Lake began to assume its present character in the early 1900s. The State Capitol and many other historic buildings were built. Electric trolleys traveled the downtown area, and their depot was in a now-popular shopping mall called Trolley Square. Original brick walls and cement floors provide a historic aura for stores, boutiques, restaurants and movie theaters.

The State Capitol Building itself, presiding over the city to the north, is worth a visit, particularly when the Utah Legislature is not in session and parking is more readily available. The building, constructed of native granite, houses exhibits from all of the state's 29 counties. Directly to the north of the capitol itself is the State Office Building, built in the 1950s as an office annex. Since that time, the increasing size of state government has necessitated the construction of a number of other state office buildings situated strategically around Salt Lake Valley.

The trolleys were replaced in the 1930s by buses, and the last streetcar line was discontinued in 1941. However, with the explosion of cars and people, state leaders decided in the late 1990s to build a $312 million light rail system, known as TRAXX, to transport people north and south along the valley corridor. Train tracks were embedded in the asphalt on some busy streets when the TRAXX north-south line was implemented at the end of 1999. The east-west extensions of the light rail system will ultimately carry passengers from Salt Lake International Airport to the University of Utah east of the city.

The city skyline began changing quite dramatically in the 1960s, when the Salt Palace convention center was built in the downtown area. In the outskirts, several commercial and service centers were being constructed to lure residents to stay in their suburbs to shop. In order to draw them back downtown, the Mormon Church invested $40 million in the development of the ZCMI Center—a mall named for Zion's Cooperative Mercantile Institution. That store, which originated in pioneer times, is sometimes called the first department store in the United States.

As the years wore into the 1970s, new downtown businesses were built along with another mall,

Crossroads, which is located just across the street from Temple Square. The 1980s saw an expansion of the Salt Palace, and the origination of several other centers including the Salt Lake International Center near the airport, the University of Utah Research Park, the Triad Center, and the Delta Center, home of the Utah Jazz.

The Salt Palace was again under the hammer in the 1990s when it was completely demolished and rebuilt to accommodate even larger groups. Gone was the original white-drum structure that had become a unique part of Salt Lake's downtown skyline, having been deemed unlikely to withstand a major earthquake. Major office towers and a new court complex were also built. The airport saw the addition of a new runway to accommodate increasing air travel, and a large new parking terrace. Plans are under way for even yet another addition to the increasingly busy airport.

Sightseers may enjoy a plethora of other destinations downtown. The Salt Lake Art Center, Abravanel Concert Hall, the Hansen Planetarium, historic Temple Square, the LDS Family History Museum, the Capitol Theatre and several museums are within walking distance of one another. The world famous Mormon Tabernacle Choir practices weekly in the Tabernacle on Temple Square when the group is not on tour. Rehearsals are most Thursdays at 8 p.m., while live broadcasts are every Sunday morning at 9:30. The Tabernacle Choir was founded in the 1860s as the official choir of the Mormon Church. Its Sunday program of "Music and the Spoken Word" has been broadcast weekly since 1929 over the Columbia Broadcasting System "from the crossroads of the west" as the weekly script tells the listener.

Recitals on the renowned Tabernacle organ are also held. The neighboring Assembly Hall, also on Temple Square, hosts a variety of vocal and instrumental concerts on Friday and Saturday evenings throughout the year.

Abravanel Hall was named for European immigrant orchestra conductor Maurice Abravanel, who came to Utah in 1947 and built the Utah Symphony into a world-class orchestra. Unlike most music halls, Abravanel Hall was designed by an acoustical engineer, helped by an architect, rather than the other way around. Before the hall was completed, the orchestra had played in the Tabernacle on Temple Square for many years.

A number of parks, the Hogle Zoo, historic churches, museums and gardens are spread throughout the valley. Liberty Park, set in a residential area near downtown, includes four square city blocks, and the Tracy Aviary. One significant state park is the "This is the Place Heritage Monument," so named for being the spot where Brigham Young stood in 1847. From this point, Young looked out at the valley for the first time, having traveled 1,300 miles west with fellow pioneers.

Spread Eagle Peak, Middle Basin, Uinta Mountain Wilderness

Indian paintbrush and lupin in the Emerald Lake area

Mount Agassiz, Middle Basin, Uinta Mountain Wilderness

The Utah Museum of Natural History on the University of Utah campus allows visitors to experience 200 million years under one roof. One may walk through time looking at Jurassic dinosaurs and Native American artifacts, many of which were found in Utah. Red Butte Gardens, a beautiful botanical garden located on the east side of the Salt Lake Valley, is a popular venue for social events year-round.

Diverse landscapes sit on either side of Salt Lake City, east and west. To the west there is flat desert that stretches into Nevada. To the east, rugged mountains rise up – the remnants of prehistoric glacial activity.

Rising east of Salt Lake and running north and south is the Wasatch Mountain Range, considered the western-most range of the Rocky Mountain system. It is approximately 150 miles in length, and its widest section is the portion on the eastern border of Salt Lake. Altitudes range from 5,000 feet to 11,000 feet in a range of topographic features created by glacial and stream activity including cirques, moraines, and hanging valleys.

These valleys provide convenient but tranquil getaways for residents and visitors: skiing in the winter, hiking and picnicking in the summer. From north to south the canyons opening onto the Salt Lake Valley include City Creek, Red Butte, Emigration, Parley's, Mill Creek, Big Cottonwood and Little Cottonwood. Most lie within the Wasatch-Cache National Forest.

A third geologic feature that defines northern Utah is called the Basin and Range province. The desert area lies generally west of Salt Lake and is characterized by short mountain ranges bounded by faults and surrounded by alluvium-filled valleys.

Northern Utah

In terms of orientation, Salt Lake is near the north end of the state. The state was colonized along the corridor that now serves as Interstate 15. In general terms, that highway runs north to Idaho and south to Nevada. As decades passed, off-shoots to that corridor allowed development in other reaches of the state. But cities along I-15 continue to see the most population growth in the state.

The northernmost major city in Utah is Logan, home to Utah State University. It is a high mountain valley known for dairy and other agricultural production. Winter finds a valley full of snow and some of the coldest temperatures in the state, due to a "cold sink" effect that occurs. Summers are delightful, as temperatures are cool and the valley is a verdant carpet. A drive through a short mountain pass takes travelers to Bear Lake, a favorite spot for summer boaters and campers. The lake straddles the Utah-Idaho border. It is also near the Wyoming state line. The small town of Garden City has made a seasonal industry out of raspberry production from the numerous bushes that grow in the mountain climate. Statewide, Bear Lake raspberries are famous in milk shakes, pies and delicious raspberry jam.

The drive from Logan south to Salt Lake City will take the traveler along a corridor that runs between the shores of the Great Salt Lake and the Wasatch Mountains. It will pass by and through parts of Brigham City, where the traveler may head northwest to the Golden Spike National Historic Site.

Promontory Point is where the famous golden spike was driven into the rails to mark the spot where construction from east and west met. This joining in 1869 created the first transcontinental railway in the United States, as the Union Pacific and Central Pacific joined hands. Shortly after completion of the line other railways were built, providing a network across much of the state. The Golden Spike National Historic Site is near Interstate 84, one of two major thoroughfares that take travelers from Utah into Idaho (the other being Interstate 15).

Also in northern Utah is the Hyrum State Park where one may enjoy boating, year-round fishing, water skiing, camping and swimming at this 450-acre lake. This park is located less than 15 minutes from Logan. The park is about 16 miles away from Hardware Ranch, which is a winter wildlife feeding ranch in the Blacksmith Fork Canyon.

The next well-known city heading south is Brigham City which is supported by an economic mix that includes defense contractors and farmers. Named for Brigham Young, the city was the first working

Beautiful snow-covered Red Canyon

Golden Spike Historic Site, Promontory

model of self-sufficiency in a church-ordered effort toward independence.

Visitors can drive "Utah's Fruitway," Highway 89 as it traverses the foothills through orchard lands. Farmers planted stands of fruit trees in these higher areas to avoid the early frosts of spring and late frosts of fall. Although all types of fruit trees are grown here – apple, plum, and pear – it is peaches that are famous in Brigham City. The annual Peach Days celebration is held here in September. Its history is tied to the mid-1850s when a man named William Wrighton purchased 100 peach stones from a Salt Lake City shop for $1 and returned to Brigham City to plant them. While many others talked of planting corn and potatoes, he dreamed of fruit trees. His dream came true.

A "hot spot" north of Brigham City is Crystal Hot Springs, a natural springs located between Tremonton and the Idaho state line. A family resort has been created around the springs with tent and RV camping available.

Another major city along Interstate 15 is Ogden, named for an early mountain man in the region. Peter Skene Ogden came to the area as part of an expedition with the Hudson's Bay Company, a British firm. Journals kept by Ogden's company in 1825 called the Ogden Valley a "hole" because it is surrounded by mountains. The river that flows through the valley also bears Ogden's name, while the county in which the city is located is named for another early trapper, John H. Weber.

Ogden has long been known as a "railroad town," and historically has boasted a diverse population. Visitors to Ogden's historic downtown may feel as if they have been transported to another time. The architecture and heritage of Peery's Egyptian Theater have been restored there, as have other buildings in styles reflecting the 19th century.

Don't miss a trip to Union Station on Wall Avenue, where you may feel you have taken a train back in time. Once there visitors may enjoy the Utah State Railroad Museum, the Browning/Kimball Car Museum, and the region's visitor center. Another venue that captures the history of the Ogden area is the Eccles Dinosaur Park. It is an outdoor facility with more than 100 life-size dinosaurs, marine creatures and flying reptiles.

On the Weber State University campus, in Ogden, is The Ice Sheet where one can fancy themselves as Olympic athletes. The Ice Sheet will host skating events during the 2002 Winter Olympic Games.

Nearby, Hill Air Force Base and its F-16 fighter aircraft operation is but one of several outposts operated by the federal government. All help to provide a hefty benefit to the region's economy. For example, the Internal Revenue Service has regional offices in Ogden, as does the U.S. Forest Service. The Defense Supply Agency Depot also contributes to the economy.

Many popular state parks dot the Ogden area such as Willard Bay State Park, one of the nation's largest waterfowl bird refuges. The park is at the top of the Great Salt Lake flood plain and is a 9,900-acre body of fresh water, unlike the southern tip of the giant lake which has extremely high salinity levels. This state park provides opportunities for boating, water skiing, and year-round fishing. Another ideal park for water enthusiasts is Lost Creek State Park, 10 miles northeast of Croydon.

Fort Buenaventura State Park was the first permanent Anglo settlement in the Great Basin. The era of the mountain man, with the associated exploration, trapping and trading customs of the western United States, came to a close in this area. The fort was originally established by Miles Goodyear in the early 1840s. It has been reconstructed on 32 acres and includes stockade and cabin replicas on the original site, a visitor center, group camping, canoe rentals and day-use areas.

South of Salt Lake, but still a major city in northern Utah, is Provo. It is one of the most rapidly growing areas of the state, characterized by a high population of Mormon residents and a burgeoning computer technology industry.

Utah County, in which Provo lies, is the state's version of Silicon Valley. The plethora of young, well-educated workers is fueled by Brigham Young University, also located in Provo. The university is privately owned by the LDS Church and struggles to keep up with the demand of students wanting to attend the institution.

The topography of Utah County is varied and beautiful. The granite walls of the noble Mount Timpanogos tower above the valley, which gives way to the shores of Utah Lake, a freshwater lake that flows into the Great Salt Lake. Historically, agricultural industries were abundant in Utah County. Geneva Steel has until recent years employed a major sector of the working population here. Waning steel prices in the U.S., coupled with evermore strict environmental controls on the operation of smokestacks and other appendages of a steel plant, have taken a hit on Geneva's profitability.

Tourist attractions include the Seven Peaks Water Park and Ice Rink which offers more than 40 activities. If visitors aren't inclined to enjoy commercial water sports, they may enjoy a drive up Provo Canyon along the pristine Provo River, which has blue ribbon fishing qualities. The spectacular Bridal Veil Falls cascade down the granite cliffs in Provo Canyon, where once a tourist tram operated until it was destroyed by an avalanche. One can still enjoy a walking tour that ascends a portion of the cliff side through the mist of the falls.

Autumn aspen and flaming maples in the Uinta Mountains

The Magic of the West Desert

The arid and deserted west desert that is now crossed by Interstate 80 is a marvel due to its stark, unchanging nature. In fact, historians have documented areas where wagon wheel ruts still exist, having been left by pioneers who tried to navigate the sometimes muddy flatlands in the 1800s. Modern fame came to the desert's Salt Flats where the world's fastest ground speeds have been recorded.

The drive from Salt Lake west passes by Tooele, which like Ogden is home to substantial federal defense outposts, and on to the city of Wendover, which straddles the Utah-Nevada line. Residents of the Wasatch Front who have a hankering to try their luck may take a 90-minute drive to the gaming tables of West Wendover, Nevada.

Visitors to Tooele County may enjoy driving the Oquirrh Loop, named for the mountains that rise up to the west of the Salt Lake Valley. This loop consists of a network of Utah State Highways 36, 73, 112 and 68. One stop is the historic Benson Grist Mill near Stansbury Park, which dates to the 1850s. The Tooele County Railroad and Mining Museum offers simulated mine and railroad displays and is housed in the former Tooele Valley Railroad Depot, built in 1909.

Southeast of Tooele in the Oquirrh Mountains, visitors may catch a glimpse of a "living ghost town," when they see Ophir, where gold was discovered in 1860. A small population of current residents lives amid the ruins of a bygone mining era.

Another gold-producing area was Mercur, which is home to the Barrick Mercur Museum between Grantsville and Tooele off Highway 112. Mercur has a nickname as "the town that can't stay dead."

Skirting the southern portion of the Oquirrh Loop is the historic Pony Express Trail, now used mainly by recreationists such as endurance horseback riders who race the route. A few pony express stations remain along the infrequently traveled Pony Express Trail, which skirts the south end of Dugway Proving Grounds and the Great Salt Lake in Tooele and Juab counties.

The west desert of Utah is barren but beautiful. The name of one particular area, near Delta in the western middle section of the state, is something of an oxymoron. Topaz was named for the gems that rested underground—a contrast to the stark greasewood valleys above ground. Another contrast lies in the history of the area, and the effects of World War II.

An influx of people of Japanese descent moved to Utah during the war, before an executive order

The famous Bonneville Salt Flats at sunset

Snow-covered aspens in Dixie National Forest

required the relocation of all Pacific Coast Japanese. That order took place on March 27, 1942, and all Japanese were forced to move out of what were deemed "strategic" areas along the western U.S. coastline. Thus, about 1,500 people were moved to Utah, adding to 2,000 Japanese that had already been living here at the time.

The area of Topaz in Millard County was designated as the Central Utah War Relocation Center, and it housed more than 8,000 Japanese Americans. This "town" was one of 10 similar quasi-concentration camps established across the nation. It was comprised of tar paper barracks, and during its peak, it was the fifth most populous city in Utah.

The residents of Topaz were closely supervised during the war, and allowed to work only agricultural or other non-sensitive jobs. Needless to say, they were denied many privileges. Before the war ended, the War Relocation Authority began allowing the internees to move from relocation centers to places where jobs were available. Some didn't move very far—the Tooele Ordinance Depot became a primary employer of Japanese Americans.

Eastern Utah

East of Salt Lake City the terrain becomes dramatically vertical. All of the various canyons that deliver water to the Salt Lake Valley are quick and immediate escapes from city life. But one—Parley's Canyon—is a major artery for national east-west traffic as Interstate 80 threads its way from the Wasatch Front to the "Wasatch Back."

Although most of Utah's population growth has been in Salt Lake and the major cities to the north and south, high immigration to the state and natural growth has caused Summit and Wasatch counties on the back side of the Wasatch Mountains to boom.

Most notable is Park City—an area steeped in pioneer mining heritage and present-day notoriety connected with being an international ski destination. Park City is about 30 miles east of Salt Lake, and it boasts an eclectic center for museums, art galleries, boutiques and recreational opportunities.

Lumber and minerals first lured pioneers to the Park City area. In northern Utah, the 1870s and '80s saw an erratic period of entrepreneurial activity by individuals, some of whom were launched into Utah fame by the riches they made from ore strikes. The last decade of that century saw a stabilization in mining, with healthy markets for gold, silver, copper and lead. During this time, large-scale harvesting of salt was taking place at the Great Salt Lake, while elsewhere gypsum and sulfur were being produced.

In Park City, historic Main Street is a draw for visitors and residents who enjoy a flavor that speaks of the town's ability to have converted its historic clout into a current cosmopolitan mixture. Main Street, while not easy to navigate by car due to its incline, its narrowness, and its congestion, is still a must-see for visitors.

The popularity of downhill skiing in the 1960s and '70s pulled the small mining community from ghost-town status, and its expansion as both a resort town and bedroom community has snowballed (no pun intended).

Three major ski resorts surround the city, the core of which is nestled in an alpine box-canyon configuration. The glaciation that gave the Wasatch Mountains their character also lent itself to ski run development. The ski slopes and multi-million-dollar homes of Deer Valley look down upon the town, while Park City Mountain Resort is physically connected to the city's historic neighborhoods via a chair lift called the Town Lift. Just west of Park City proper, only a few miles away, is The Canyons, which

Jones Hole, Dinosaur National Monument

Columbines in the Uinta Mountains

Split Mountain and Green River, Dinosaur National Monument

has enjoyed tremendous and ambitious expansion since it was purchased by the American Skiing Company in the late 1990s.

Snow season is when Park City hustles and bustles the most. Late November brings World Cup ski racing, while January sees an onslaught of Hollywood luminaries and independent film-makers who attend the world-famous Sundance Film Festival.

Though Park City seems to "blossom" the most in the winter, it has rapidly become a year-round visitor destination. What locals used to call the "shoulder seasons" in the muddy months of late spring and early fall are barely noticeable in the burgeoning tourist industry there. Summer sees several festivals, most notably a big 4th of July bash and an August art festival. Drawing from its roots as a labor town, the community celebrates Miner's Day on Labor Day each fall with a big breakfast, parade and mucking-and-drilling contests. The Alpine Slide on the grassy slopes of the lower Park City Mountain Resort gives riders a thrilling "woosh" down the mountain on sleds that travel in cement tracks.

Even when there is no special event occurring, however, visitors to Park City can enjoy several other activities. The Park City Silver Mine Adventure takes people into the bowels of the mountains that put Park City on the map. An original mine train descends 1,500 feet into an authentic silver mine that dates to the turn of the 20th century.

Recent changes to the Park City profile bespeak the coming of the 2002 Winter Olympic Games. Just west of town on State Road 224 is the gateway to the Winter Sports Park, which is home to several ski jumps, a luge track and bobsled run. Those of the public who wish to get a feel for what an Olympic athlete faces during competition may do so in limited recreational programs offered by the park. Likewise, some of the same ski slopes that are used by World Cup ski competitions—and that will be used for the Olympics—are open for use by recreational skiers.

A little further east of Salt Lake is Wasatch County and the cities of Heber and Midway. This alpine valley is verdant in the summer, and its heritage as being settled by Scandinavian immigrants is evident in chalet-styled homes and the annual Swiss Days celebration.

Midway will host the Nordic venue for the Olympics. Its gentle valley floor accommodates cross-country skiers in the winter, while the summer time sees agricultural activity. Midway has been known for decades for its delightful hot springs that bubble to the surface, offering those who take a dip the opportunity to relax and hope to heal their bodies with the mineral-filled waters. A landmark on the historic Homestead Resort is a huge hot springs crater which feeds spas at the resort. In the winter, visitors may enjoy sleigh rides and snowmobiling, while golf is a popular sport in the summer.

The Homestead has its own 18-hole course, while nearby Wasatch Mountain State Park—the busiest in Utah's state park system—boasts three nine-hole courses.

Busy U.S. Highway 40 serves Summit and Wasatch Counties, extending into Utah's Uintah Basin to the east. The Uintah Basin is famous for oil and gas production. Vernal and Roosevelt are its major communities, although many other smaller towns exist throughout the area to serve a rich agricultural economy. Vernal is also Utah's gateway to Flaming Gorge Dam and Reservoir to the north, where a massive dam on the Green River has created one of the state's most beautiful and popular large bodies of water. Just east of Vernal, near the Green River community of Jensen is the famed Dinosaur Quarry in Dinosaur National Monument, where visitors can observe scientists unearthing the remains of the giant animals that roamed the once tropical swamps of what would become eastern Utah.

The Virgin River in Zion Canyon, Zion National Park

Opposite: Towers of the Virgins, Zion National Park

Central Utah

The south central part of Utah is served by U. S. Highway 89, which passes through pastoral valleys and pioneer communities that still thrive on an agriculturally-based economy. The community of Mt. Pleasant is the home of Wasatch Academy, a private church-operated school that has a long and rich history.

To the south of Mt. Pleasant is Manti, which is the home of the LDS Manti Temple, probably one of the oldest such structures built by Mormon colonists after they first began settling the rich farming valleys to the south of the Wasatch Front. LDS religious faithful flock to Manti each June to view the Mormon Miracle Pageant, now in its fourth decade of existence. The outdoor play tells the story of how church leader Joseph Smith had his "great awakening." The story follows the Mormons through their years of persecution and how this budding new American church moved from New York to Ohio, then Missouri and eventually to Utah. The pageant is enacted at night on a hill overlooking the Sanpete Valley. The Manti Temple serves as a backdrop, and the soundtrack to the play is performed by the Mormon Tabernacle Choir and other church organizations.

Pre-pageant celebration includes a delicious turkey dinner at the local churches. An unusual marinade of lemon-lime soda and soy sauce are the ingredients for this flavorful turkey. Central Utah valleys are well-known for the production of turkeys. The community of Moroni and its turkey processing facility, is central to that industry, and communities for miles around are marked by low-lying turkey sheds housing the thousands of birds that ultimately find their way to dinner tables all over the nation.

Richfield, located in Sevier County, is the bustling hub city of central Utah.

Near the eastern center of the state is the city of Price. It is distinguished by two major features: vast coal reserves, and the most ethnically diverse community in the state. The two features are intertwined, however, as it was the lure of coal mining in the late 1800s that brought Greeks, Italians, Yugoslavs, Czechs, Mexicans, Japanese, Chinese, Russians and Germans to the area. In 1920, thirty-three different nationalities resided in the Price area. Consequently, the religious mix in the Price area is equally diverse.

Not surprisingly, Price has been a black sheep in terms of Utah politics throughout history. It is a bastion of the Democratic Party in an otherwise Republican-dominated state.

The name of the city goes back to 1869, when Mormon bishop William Price led an expedition from

Utah Valley (the southern end of the Wasatch Front) through Spanish Fork Canyon. The fertile valley surrounding the Price River was ideal for farming and ranching. It was not until the next decade, in 1877, that mining took precedence over farming in terms of industrial development.

Initial coal mining was on a small scale. But in 1883, the Denver & Rio Grande Western Railroad put down tracks through the valley as part of a Denver-to-Salt Lake City route. Immigrant laborers were aboard these trains, and many got off at Price to work in the coal mines.

Just north of Price is a small town named Helper, so named for the locomotives that were added on at this juncture to "help" push heavy trains over Soldier Summit, a mountain saddle in Spanish Fork Canyon.

A major earth slide in Spanish Fork Canyon in 1953 inundated the small town of Thistle, and resulted in the rebuilding of the railroad and U.S. Highway 6.

The history of Price, as in Park City and other mining towns, is dotted with its share of tragedies related to the dangers of mineral extraction. Explosions, cave-ins, floods and fires were common.

Even though mining operations in Price peaked in 1940, the industry is still a mainstay for Carbon and Emery counties. Advances in technology, particularly related to the relatively new longwall mining machine, have drastically cut down on the number of people required to do the job.

Although Price is more than 100 miles away from the Wasatch Front, opportunities for higher learning are available to residents here. The College of Eastern Utah serves a student body largely comprised of regional residents and has satellite campuses throughout southeastern Utah. It is distinguished by having the first black female college president in Utah—Dr. Grace Sawyer Jones—who was hired in 1996. Another distinguishing feature is the Prehistoric Museum at CEU, which boasts the largest collection of dinosaur tracks in the world.

The natural features of the landscape surrounding Price show a transition of land forms, as the foothills of the northern Utah mountains give way to the Colorado Plateau.

As travelers head east and south on Highway 191 they begin to enter the "Dinosaur Diamond," a large area in the central and southeastern portion of the state. The Cleveland-Lloyd Dinosaur Quarry near Price, Dinosaur National Monument near Vernal, and the Mill Canyon dinosaur trail near Moab offer modern man a glimpse into prehistoric life.

What a person sees in these landscapes now is very different than when the great beasts roamed the land. Today the landscape is barren and eroded. But during the Jurassic period 150 million years ago the climates were mild and moist, as evidenced by looking at the geologic Morrison Formation. This formation, comprised of layers of clay, shale and sandstone, has provided a resting place for the fossilized

The Pink Cliffs near Cascade Falls

Fisher's Towers, Castle Valley, La Sal Mountains

remnants of dinosaurs and plants. Common inhabitants at the time included Allosaurus, Camptosaurus, Stegosaurus and Camarasaurus.

Jurassic period geology is clearly visible in multi-colored layers of rock in southeastern Utah. The forces of water and wind-blown sand and silt created layers of sandstone. For example, the Navajo sandstone overlays the late Triassic Kayenta and Wingate sandstones, and the Entrada sandstone that is the hallmark of rock formations in Arches National Park near Moab.

The settlement of the southeastern portion of the state came later than that which occurred along the Interstate 15 corridor. This region presented difficulties for travelers, and Native American Indians who inhabited the area first were not pleased to have neighbors.

But encroachment and settlement of the white man did occur. However, it was not until the late 1860s that people other than non-Mormons began developing internal transportation networks. It was the lure of mining that caused this interest in accessing outlying areas, such as Carbon and Emery counties in southeastern Utah which are famous for coal production.

Autumn in Christmas Meadow, Uinta Mountains

Dirty Devil River, Lake Powell area

Balanced Rock, Arches National Park

Moab and La Sal Mountains from Dead Horse Point

Delicate Arch, Arches National Park near Moab

Bull moose enjoying a cool breakfast in Uinta National Forest

Opposite: Mustard seed in bloom near Midway

Hayden Peak, Butterfly Lake, Uinta Mountains

Winter at Tate Barn area of Heber Valley, site of Olympic cross-country skiing venue

Autumn beauty in North Fork Canyon

Former Mormon settlement near Fruita

Opposite: The Castle, Capitol Reef National Park

Valley of the Gods near Blanding

Lake Powell, Glen Canyon National Recreational Area

Thor's Hammer at Sunrise Point, Bryce Canyon National Park

Bison and friends at Antelope Island State Park

Washer Woman Arch, Island in the Sky, Canyonlands National Park

Southern Utah

The southern portion of Utah is home to five national parks which dot the bottom of the state from west to east. In broad terms, this area is part of the Colorado Plateau, bordered on the south by the Sonoran and Painted Desert, on the west by Nevada's Great Basin, on the east by the Rocky Mountains, and on the north by the Uinta Mountains.

In terms of orientation, continuing through the southeastern area of the state where dinosaurs once roamed, the visitor next comes to Moab, which is located some 30 miles south of the Crescent Junction exit from Interstate 70 on U.S. Highway 191.

Arches National Park, just a few miles north of Moab, is home to the greatest number of natural stone spans in the world. It also is home to Delicate Arch, which in many respects is an icon for the state. Its image is frequently used in television advertisements, on vehicle license plates, and a model of its image was part of the celebration decorations when Salt Lake City was awarded the bid to host the 2002 Winter Olympic Games.

Those wishing to view the 46-foot-tall by 35-foot-wide arch may do so by taking a 2-mile hike, or they can drive to a vantage point below the slickrock bowl over which Delicate Arch towers. It is but one of many outstanding features, including one of the world's longest natural stone arches—Landscape Arch. Fiery Furnace, Courthouse Towers, the Three Gossips, Devils Garden, the Parade of Elephants, the Tower of Babel and Park Avenue are all images that give animation to their stony structure.

The geologic history of Arches is one founded in salt. Geologists have found that sandstone spans began forming 300 million years ago in the Pennsylvanian period, when saltwater from a prehistoric ocean flooded the area. Debris later covered these layers of saline deposits, which was then gradually compressed into rock. The weight of the rock caused the salt to seep out, creating faults, domes and anticlines. Other sediments were deposited, then erosion occurred via wind and water.

Also near Moab is Canyonlands—Utah's largest national park. It is comprised of three districts—Needles, Island in the Sky and The Maze.

Needles is in the southeastern section of the park. The sandstone formations for which this district is named stand in upright formations, tinged in various shades of red, orange and rust. Most of Canyonlands is accessible only by four-wheel drive and on foot.

In many canyons of this area, petroglyphs and pictographs have been left behind by prehistoric peoples. One tight cluster of petroglyphs is near the entrance to the Needles District. It is Newspaper Rock Recreation Site, located 13 miles off U.S. Highway 191 on U-211. The images pecked into the rock face reveal 1,000 years of communication, from the prehistoric Indians through the early Utes and white settlers.

The Maze section is in the westernmost part of Canyonlands. It is extremely remote and rugged and has been described as "a 30-square-mile puzzle in sandstone." Notable features are the Land of Standing Rocks, the Doll House and the Fins.

Island in the Sky is an easy drive north from Moab. Its name probably reflects the fact that the broad, level mesa is the highest section of Canyonlands. It is literally a peninsula in the sky, bordered on the west by the Green River and on the east by the Colorado River. One peculiar feature is Upheaval Dome, which resembles a meteor crater. Scientists have not been able to determine its origin. The overlook at Grand View Point of Island in the Sky offers breathtaking views over 100 miles away, as well as the sandstone bench called the White Rim that follows the contours of the mesa far below.

The 100-mile-long road that traverses the White Rim is within park boundaries. It is popular for mountain biking but those camping overnight must first have a permit to do so, which in many cases can take weeks or months to obtain.

Below the White Rim, the Green and Colorado rivers meet, then flow through the popular white water section known as Cataract Canyon. From there, the waters empty into Lake Powell, flow through Glen Canyon Dam to the Grand Canyon, and out to the sea at the Gulf of California.

Near Island in the Sky is Dead Horse Point State Park. There is no live water on this high mesa, which was used near the turn of the century by cowboys who could herd livestock onto the tip of the area in a sort of corral. A narrow strip of land called "the neck" connects the broader mesa with the tip, now called Dead Horse Point. It was named many decades ago after a band of horses was inadvertently left there for so long that they died of thirst. This state park offers exhilarating views of Canyonlands and the Colorado River 2,000 feet below, and the La Sal Mountains whose peaks rise to nearly 13,000 feet. President Lyndon B. Johnson signed legislation in 1964 preserving Canyonlands as a national park.

The city of Moab has a history tied to mining, but the minerals that were rich in this country were not needed for making steel or jewelry. In the 1950s and '60s, the demand for uranium grew as a source for making weapons. Prospectors made their fortunes and lost their shirts mining uranium in the areas

Autumn aspen grove, Dixie National Forest

Autumn cottonwoods, Capitol Reef National Park

Bridal Veil Falls, Provo River Canyon

surrounding Moab. A mill, near the banks of the Colorado River which cuts across the Moab Valley, thrived from the late '50s through the '70s, but the industry went bust just as the cold war did.

Tourism bailed the community out of its recession, thanks to the surrounding parks and the popularity of mountain biking and river rafting. Numerous mountain bike trails lead out of town, and just a few miles away is the Slickrock Trail, where riders can take their mountain bikes and motorcycles on a natural roller coaster of sandstone fins.

To the west of Canyonlands on Highway 24 is Capitol Reef National Park, home to an outstanding feature called Waterpocket Fold. It is a 100-mile-long "fold" in the crust of the earth carved by deep canyons. Rock art left by the Fremont Indian culture dots the sandstone walls here.

Capitol Reef takes its name from two sources. The "reef" describes a barrier-type ridge of rock, and the "capitol" is named for the striking white, domed sandstone peaks that top the rock formations. One area is called Egyptian Temple, while others such as Golden Throne, Chimney Rock and Capitol Dome reflect man-made images for which they are named.

Geologists would describe Waterpocket Fold as a classic monocline, formed between 50 million and 70 million years ago. Layers of rock exhibit signs that a major geologic shift took place in western North America and an ancient buried fault was reactivated. The rock layers were pushed, bent and pressured. The sediments that were shifted during this episode, however, range in age from the Permian to Cretaceous periods, spanning 200 million years of time. After the "fold" occurred, erosion carved up the landscape even more.

The term "pocket" in the area's name comes from the natural basins which can hold thousands of gallons of rainwater. Since the area is a remote desert, these pockets of water allowed humans to live there, in addition to fresh supplies from Sulphur Creek and the Fremont River. Thus, there are traces of the Fremont culture of American Indians that date to 700 A.D., but vanished in about 1300 A.D. Historians speculate that drought made it impossible to live there for a prolonged time.

Mormon settlers came to the area in 1880, and residents made healthy agricultural livelihoods in the area until the late 1960s. Congress designated Capitol Reef a national park in 1971, but an abundant orchard near the visitor's center is evidence of the area's history.

While Capitol Reef is easily accessed by car, there are remote areas such as Cathedral Valley, Muley Twist Canyon and Brimhall Bridge. These areas offer fine hiking experiences, but the trailheads are accessed via dirt roads which often require four-wheel drive.

Bryce Canyon is the next national park in the string of beauties that dot lower Utah. The hallmarks of this park are the thousands of spires that stand upright like needles, having been created by strong erosion. Paiute lore calls the tall, slender pillars with nearly glowing tips "the Legend People" who were turned to stone by an angry god. The Claron Formation of rock reveals 60 million years of history, which is relatively recent on the geologic scale. These formations took shape during the late Cretaceous period, also known as the Reptile Age, when flowering plants appeared and dinosaurs disappeared.

The name of the park stems from an early livestock man who grazed cattle amongst the fins in the early 1870s. Ebenezer Bryce was a Scottish immigrant and early settler of the area. While his cattle found forage on the plateau adjacent to Bryce Canyon, he dreaded when they wandered away. He coined the oft-used phrase that the canyon was "a heck of a place to lose a cow."

Nowadays, the only livestock in Bryce Canyon are horses availing visitors a break from hiking into the gorge. The two-hour or half-day trips are reminiscent of mini-versions of riding into the Grand Canyon.

Visitors may also take a 35-mile round-trip drive to the various vistas of the park. Famous overlooks include Fairyland View, Pariah View, and Sunrise, Sunset, Inspiration and Bryce points. For long-distance views, the points named Farview, Rainbow and Yovimpa are breathtaking.

The rustic Bryce Canyon Lodge, which offers a full range of visitor services, is on the National Register of Historic Places.

The next major stop in southern Utah on the national park tour is Zion whose geologic history began 225 million years ago. Visitors can see layers of rock that tell a history of once being the floor of a shallow sea, then the delta of a river, then the bottom of a lake. Volcanic matter and wind-blown sand provided sediment that at first were dunes, then later were severely compacted into sandstone. Other layers covered these (some of which have already eroded away). Geologists note that in comparison with the rock formations in Utah's other national parks, Zion is fairly young. Erosive forces cause the geology to be in a constant state of change.

Another force that helped create Zion was a lengthy uplifting of the Colorado Plateau, which was cut by streams to create spectacular canyons. The most notable stream in the area is the Virgin River, which meets the mighty Colorado at Lake Mead.

The name of the park has historic significance tied to Mormon pioneers who settled the area. Mormons who fled eastern states in the mid-1800s were searching for their own "Zion" as characterized by Jewish culture. After settling the Salt Lake Valley and spreading into southern Utah, the grandeur of what is now called Zion National Park elicited feelings of reverence to the pioneers.

The theme is repeated as evidenced by the names of individual landmarks within the park: Angel's

White Canyon, Natural Bridges State Park

Slot Canyon, Buckskin Gulch, Paria Wilderness Area

Opposite: Calf Creek Falls, Escalante Valley

Landing, the Great White Throne, Altar of Sacrifice, the West Temple, and the Three Patriarchs (Abraham, Isaac and Jacob).

The sacred nature of the park did not go unnoticed by even earlier inhabitants. Legend has it that Southern Paiute people believed spirits roamed around the rock formations. Even earlier inhabitants may have felt the same way, but there is no record of their thoughts. Historians have found remnants of a civilization that dates to 285 A.D.

The Mormon explorers who came to the southwestern corner of the state were not in search of recreation areas, as visitors are today. These original white settlers were sent by Brigham Young to find a climate suitable for growing cotton. In the church's quest to become entirely self-sufficient, pioneers settled other areas to develop natural resources that would fulfill this mission. For example, Iron County near the southwest corner of the state is named for the extraction of iron in the ground with which to make steel.

Snuggled in the southwest corner of the state is Washington County, which has long been known as "Utah's Dixie." The quest to grow cotton was fueled by a deficiency of the plant due to the Civil War. The county seat is St. George, a burgeoning playground of golf courses, hotels and spas located in a red rock valley that hosts the only climate in the state where palm trees can grow. The St. George area is one of Utah's fastest growing, as newcomers flock there to make their homes in the mild year-round climate.

Descriptions of Utah's national parks paint a pretty dry picture. But the few waterways that flow across the Colorado Plateau are prized for their ability to sustain the health and recreational needs of many populations.

In southern Utah, most water channels are tied to the Colorado River. The Green River, which enters the eastern side of the state north of where the Colorado does, has provided boating pleasures for hundreds of years. The Price River, mentioned earlier, flows into the Green.

Early Spanish Fathers Dominguez and Escalante are the first explorers in recorded history to have their names associated with these rivers. In 1776 , on their way from Santa Fe, New Mexico to California, they crossed the Colorado River at a section that is now under the waters of Lake Powell, which is really a man-made reservoir. This historic portion of their journey was named the "Crossing of the Fathers."

Mountain men such as Jedediah Smith and Denis Julien also traveled the waterways in their quest to trap beaver. Julien, in fact, left an inscription on a rock in Cataract Canyon, now popular as a hair-raising white water rafting area.

Of all the men who took early expeditions into this untamed country, however, it was Major John Wesley Powell who is the most notorious. In 1866, and later in 1871-72, he traveled the length of the Green and Colorado rivers, in an unprecedented journey during which he mapped these inland waterways. He and his team named many mountains and rock formations that dot the landscape along the way.

Powell, who died in 1902, was a symbol of grit and courage. He lost an arm at Shiloh, commanding a battery at the heart of the hottest fighting. Then, his stump barely healed, he fought on through Vicksburg and Atlanta.

Powell came west as part of an early survey of the Southern Paiute country in southwestern Utah, and in an effort to move the Native Americans into the Uintah Basin on the eastern side of the state. The Paiutes were reluctant; however, white pressure did eventually force them to move. Those that didn't go to the Uintah Basin drifted to the Moapa Reservation in southern Nevada.

By and large, Powell was a friend to the Indians. Although some white men were killed by Indians during this period (generally because the natives feared trouble-making prospectors) Powell made alliances with them. He had Hopi and Navajo contacts, and developed a knowledge of native cultures. This background later influenced his appointment as director of the United States Bureau of Ethnology.

Powell's belief that the Colorado River deserved further exploration led him to persuade Congress to appropriate $25,000 for his later exploration. Other surveys of the greater southern Utah region were already being conducted with federal funds.

Powell finished his survey of the Colorado Plateau in 1879, providing labels and boundaries for what had been a virtually unknown land. The famed former army officer and noted explorer, later became director of the U. S. Geological Survey.

The popular Lake Powell and The John Wesley Powell River History Museum are named for Major Powell. The museum is located in Green River, just off Interstate 70 in southeastern Utah. The small city of Green River has also become associated with excellent melons of all varieties. The combination of the alkaline soil and summer temperatures provides ideal growing conditions, and several new varieties have been developed by growers in the Green River area. Melon Days is an annual event in September when visitors can eat their fill of melons, free of charge, and enjoy a day's festivities including a parade and square dance.

There are many outfitters who can provide visitors with the river experiences that early adventurers enjoyed. Sections of the Colorado, Green, San Juan, Yampa and Dolores rivers offer a variety of experiences from calm to rough water.

Superior Mountain, Little Cottonwood Canyon near Alta

Colorful hot-air balloon over Park City ski area

All of these rivers drain from the Colorado Plateau in the southeastern portion of the state. Melting snow in spring gives thrill seekers the pinnacle of entertainment when rivers rise and flow rapidly. Most popular are the high-water months of May and June, when the rivers usually overflow with snowmelt from the Rocky Mountains.

The Green and San Juan rivers are the major tributaries in Utah which flow into the mighty Colorado. The Yampa flows out of western Colorado through Dinosaur National Monument and joins the Green at Echo Park, near Vernal. The Dolores River originates in the San Juan Mountains of southwestern Colorado, and flows north along the eastern edge of the La Sal Mountains east of Moab before meeting the Colorado River about 60 miles away.

The rivers have moods. The temperament of a calm, flat stretch can change radically around the bend as water flows over huge, ancient boulders that cause the whitewater.

For the most part in the remote river canyons, there is more evidence of prehistoric civilizations than modern man. Indian ruins can be spotted on high cliffs and in rocky crags. Pictographs and petroglyphs art adorn the walls. A study of the designs conjures up thoughts about the life and culture of these early peoples. Strict laws that govern modern-day use of the rivers and canyons help ensure that today's travelers leave no traces from their journeys.

Speaking of journeys, this brief description of Utah is about to conclude. The magnitude of the state's wonders can in no way be fully covered among these few pages. It is hoped that this book will serve as a launch pad for individual discoveries of Utah's rich cultures and wealth of scenery. The state's attractions are such that only personal exploration can provide the adventures awaiting those who wish to delve further. Do come and see for yourself!

About the Photographer

A native of Michigan, photographer David C. Schultz moved to Dallas at the age of twenty-two and began his career as a fashion photographer, which he did for seven years. After visiting Utah on assignment in 1987, he returned to Dallas, closed his studio, and a month later moved to the Alpine Valley of Heber, where he currently resides.

Since moving to Utah, David has concentrated on photographing travel and landscape images and his work has appeared in such publications as *Travel & Leisure*, *Snow Country*, *Islands* and *National Geographic Traveler*. "The images of Utah are but a fraction of nature's beauty that I've been fortunate enough to witness. A very important part of photography, besides the appropriate equipment to record the moment, is the ability to see the moment, having the patience and tenacity to wait and observe the light and shadows."

In 1998, David opened his own gallery in Park City, "West Light Images," where limited edition prints of his favorite images are available.

About the Author

Sena T. Flanders is a fifth-generation native of Utah. She was born and raised in Moab, where her family has owned and operated *The Times-Independent* weekly newspaper since 1911. She received a bachelors degree in Journalism Mass Communications from the University of Utah. After graduating, she moved to Park City where she lived for 11 years, seven of which she spent as a reporter for *The Park Record* newspaper, and three as editor. She and her family moved back to the sunny weather of Moab in 1997. She currently is associate editor of *The Times-Independent*.

Glen Canyon and Colorado River

Back Cover: Bridge Mountain, Zion National Park